KELLY LEE CULBRETH

101 Fun Facts About Nashville, TN

Discovering Music City One Fascinating Story at a Time

First published by 401 Publishing 2023

Copyright © 2023 by Kelly Lee Culbreth

All rights reserved. No part of this publication may be reproduced, stored or transmitted in any form or by any means, electronic, mechanical, photocopying, recording, scanning, or otherwise without written permission from the publisher. It is illegal to copy this book, post it to a website, or distribute it by any other means without permission.

Kelly Lee Culbreth asserts the moral right to be identified as the author of this work.

Kelly Lee Culbreth has no responsibility for the persistence or accuracy of URLs for external or third-party Internet Websites referred to in this publication and does not guarantee that any content on such Websites is, or will remain, accurate or appropriate.

Designations used by companies to distinguish their products are often claimed as trademarks. All brand names and product names used in this book and on its cover are trade names, service marks, trademarks and registered trademarks of their respective owners. The publishers and the book are not associated with any product or vendor mentioned in this book. None of the companies referenced within the book have endorsed the book.

First edition

This book was professionally typeset on Reedsy.
Find out more at reedsy.com

Don't just be a Dreamer... be a Doer too!

Kelly Lee Culbreth

Contents

1	Introduction	1
2	FUN FACTS ABOUT... Nashville's History	4
3	FUN FACTS ABOUT... The Recording Industry & Music Row	10
4	FUN FACTS ABOUT... The Ryman Auditorium	15
5	FUN FACTS ABOUT... The Grand Ole Opry & Opryland Hotel	22
6	FUN FACTS ABOUT... The Bluebird Cafe	28
7	FUN FACTS ABOUT... Printer's Alley	33
8	FUN FACTS ABOUT... The Country Music Hall of Fame and Museum	38
9	FUN FACTS ABOUT... Lower Broadway	44
10	FUN FACTS ABOUT... Other Music Venues	50
11	FUN FACTS ABOUT... Things-To-Do	56
12	FUN FACTS ABOUT... Annual Events	63
13	FUN FACTS ABOUT... Food & Restaurants	69
14	FUN FACTS ABOUT... Sports in Nashville	76
15	FUN FACTS ABOUT... Bridgestone Arena	82
16	FUN FACTS ABOUT... Nissan Stadium	87
17	FUN FACTS ABOUT... Music City Center	92
18	FUN FACTS ABOUT... Landmarks	99
19	FUN FACTS ABOUT... Downtown Nashville	106
20	FUN FACTS ABOUT... Nashville Universities	112
21	FUN FACTS ABOUT... Miscellaneous Stuff	118

22	Miscellaneous Photos	123
23	Conclusion	132
24	References	134

1

Introduction

Welcome and enjoy as I take you on a journey to Nashville, TN - one fun fact at a time.

Evening roof-top view of Nashville's skyline – Photo Credit: Kelly Lee Culbreth

I first moved to the Middle Tennessee area in 1994 to attend Middle Tennessee State University. My degree was in Mass Communications, with an emphasis on the Recording Industry. I loved it here so much that I stayed, built a home, started a business, got into real estate, and became an author. Over the last 30 years, I have watched Nashville grow from a quaint, southern city to a bustling metropolis. With a HUGE, eclectic music scene, professional sports teams, and a happening nightlife, it is no wonder Nashville has become such a popular tourist destination! And because I have grown to love this city so much, I couldn't wait to compile these fun facts to share with you.

With a rich history and diverse culture, Nashville, TN is a fascinating city. There is so much to learn and love about this southern gem. And although it is impossible to cover everything there is to know about Nashville, this pocket-sized book is an excellent start in getting to know this city a little better.

Whether you are a local to the area, planning a visit, or admiring from a distance, this book will leave you just a little bit more "in the know" about the city famously known as Music City, USA.

Speaking of nicknames for Nashville, let's get this book started with...

INTRODUCTION

FUN FACT #1:

This thriving metropolis has earned quite a few nicknames over the years. Here are a few of the monikers local Nashvillians have used to refer to their city.

1. Music City, USA
2. Athens of the South
3. The Buckle on the Bible Belt
4. NashVegas
5. Cashville
6. Smashville
7. Wall Street of the South
8. Gnashville (Gnash is the beloved mascot of the Predators hockey team)
9. The Hot Chicken Capitol
10. The Birthplace of Country Music
11. Nashborough

To name a few...

* * *

2

FUN FACTS ABOUT... Nashville's History

FUN FACT #2:

Located on the Cumberland River, the area where Nashville sits today used to be a trading port.

French-Canadian explorer Martin Chartier established a trading port in 1689. Then later, in 1714, a group of French traders led by Jean du Charleville, established their trading port in this same area that soon became known as French Lick.

Although they successfully traded fur with the local Native Americans for decades, the settlement was abandoned in the 1740s.

* * *

FUN FACT #3:

The city was officially named Nashville in 1784 and became the state capital in 1843.

It wasn't until 1779 that the area formerly known as French Lick was discovered again by explorers James Robertson and John Donelson. With a group of men, they constructed Fort Nashborough.

With a great location on the Cumberland River, this settlement prospered and later shortened its name to Nashville in 1784. The city was named after American Revolutionary War hero Francis Nash.

It was in 1843 when Nashville became the capital of the State of Tennessee. With music as the main driving force behind much of its growth, this remarkable city has become one of the fastest-growing metropolitan areas in the United States.

* * *

FUN FACT #4:

Nashville's first "celebrity" was the renowned frontiersman and Congressman Davy Crockett.

Born in 1786 and known for wearing a coonskin hat, Davy Crockett grew up in East Tennessee. In 1826, he was elected to represent Tennessee in the U.S. House of Representatives.

In addition to being a politician, he was also known as a pioneer, soldier, bear hunter, and a legendary figure made famous by Walt Disney with his "Davy Crockett" TV series in 1954.

* * *

FUN FACT #5:

Due in part to the success of the Fisk Jubilee singers from Nashville's Fisk University, Nashville became a national center for music publishing in the 1800s.

Fisk Jubilee Singers in 1870's – Photo Credit: The Library of Congress

The Fisk Jubilee Singers were the first musical act to tour the world, bringing much attention to Nashville.

During a tour of Europe in 1873, the group was asked to perform for Britain's Queen Victoria, and she was quite impressed. Their efforts helped put Nashville on the map as a global music center.

* * *

FUN FACT #6:

Country Music was born in Nashville.

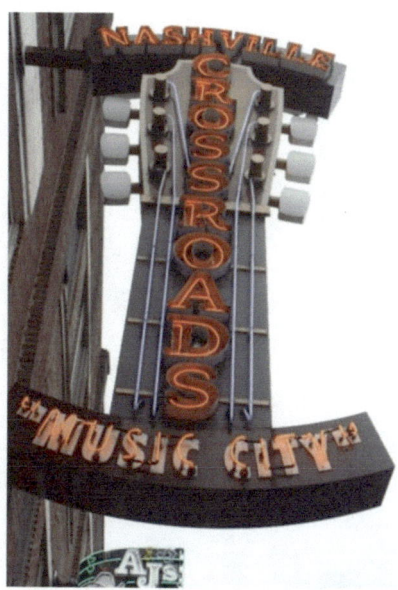

Photo Credits from left to right: Kelly Lee Culbreth & Neil Mewes

Tennessee was one of the first states in America to introduce fiddle music to the masses. When fiddles were added to gospel hymns, a new sound emerged becoming what we now call Country Music. Although Nashville is the home of Country Music, it is also known for having Christian, Gospel, Blues, R&B, Bluegrass, and Pop music scenes.

* * *

3

FUN FACTS ABOUT... The Recording Industry & Music Row

FUN FACT #7:

In 1941, Nashville was the first city in the nation to be granted an FM broadcasting license.

In the 1950s, WSM radio announcer, David Cobb, referred to Nashville as "Music City" on air for the first time. And from then on, the moniker quickly became Nashville's permanent go-to nickname.

* * *

FUN FACT #8:

Nashville is known as the "Songwriting Capital of the World."

Songwriters from around the world come to Music City to learn the art of crafting songs and to share their passion with other songwriters.

Because artists like Robert Plant, Kid Rock, Black Eyed Peas, Bon Jovi, Michael Buble, and SO MANY others have come to Nashville to write and record, Rolling Stone gave Nashville the title of the nation's "Best Music Scene" in 2011.

* * *

FUN FACT #9:

Music Row in Nashville is considered the hub of the city's entertainment industry.

ASCAP Building, 2 Music Square W, Nashville, TN - Photo Credit: Designtracs

Music Row began to develop and emerge in the 1950s. Located southwest of downtown Nashville on 16th and 17th Avenues, the area known as Music Row is full of record labels, recording studios, publishing houses, music-licensing firms, managers, video production companies, and everything related to the music business.

Over the years, upscale shops, clubs, and restaurants have also moved into the area, making Music Row a destination of its own.

* * *

FUN FACT #10:

Elvis recorded well over 200 of his songs at RCA's historic Studio B on Music Row.

Elvis Statue on Lower Broadway – Photo Credit: Mana5280

To get into the holiday spirit while working on one of his albums, Elvis put up a string of Christmas lights, which still hang in the studio to this day.

* * *

FUN FACT #11:

Nashville has the highest concentration of music industry employees anywhere in the world, at nearly 60,000.

Because Nashville is linked to music production and performance for so many different genres, this city attracts entertainment companies and artists from all over the world.

Such as Sirius XM, Gibson Brands, ASCAP, BMI, SESAC, RCA Records, Sony Music, Warner Music Group, MCA Records, Capitol Records, EMI Records, Mercury Records, Sony Music Publishing, Universal Music Publishing, and Disney Music Publishing, to name a few.

* * *

4

FUN FACTS ABOUT... The Ryman Auditorium

FUN FACT #12:

Nashville's most famous music venue was originally built as a church in 1892.

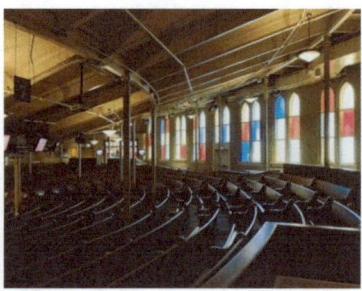

The Ryman Auditorium & the original oak pews that are still there today – Photo Credits from left to right: EQRoy & Nick Agee

Originally known as the Union Gospel Tabernacle, construction took seven years to complete.

All the pews in the Ryman Auditorium today are the original oak pews from over a hundred years ago during its days as a church.

* * *

FUN FACT #13:

The Ryman Auditorium was home to the Grand Ole Opry from 1943-1974.

At the time, the Ryman Auditorium was the largest structure of its kind in Nashville, so it quickly became the top venue for many gatherings.

After moving into the Ryman, a live radio show called the "Grand Ole Opry" gained national notoriety for having such star-studded performers every week.

Because of the Ryman's unique vibe and brilliant acoustics, for over 30 years, the Grand Ole Opry regularly performed to sold-out crowds.

***

FUN FACT #14:

The Ryman has two nicknames: "Carnegie Hall of the South" and "Mother Church of County Music."

Pollstar magazine's prestigious "Theater of the Year" award has been given to the Ryman 12 times (and counting) as the best auditorium in the nation to experience live music.

Ryman Theater & Ryman Soundboard – Photo Credits from left to right: William King & Kelly Lee Culbreth

With only 2,362 seats, unbelievable acoustics, and an intimate feel, set inside a beautiful historic theater, it's no wonder the Ryman is a favorite for music lovers and the musicians who play there.

* * *

FUN FACT #15:

In 2006, The Ryman was named the official birthplace of bluegrass music by the state of Tennessee.

A plaque outside the Ryman reads, "In December 1945, Grand Ole Opry star Bill Monroe and his mandolin brought to the Ryman Auditorium stage a band that created a new American musical form. With the banjo style of Earl Scruggs and the guitar of Lester Flatt, the new musical genre became known as 'bluegrass.'"

The combination of the mandolin, banjo, bass, fiddle, and guitar created a new sound that audiences couldn't get enough of. And bluegrass music was born at the Ryman.

* * *

FUN FACT #16:

Johnny Cash and June Carter met at the Ryman Auditorium.

In 1956, the famous couple bumped into each other backstage. But this wasn't just any night at the Ryman; that particular evening was Johnny's Grand Ole Opry debut.

That night after his performance, Johnny told June that he would marry her someday.

* * *

FUN FACTS ABOUT... THE RYMAN AUDITORIUM

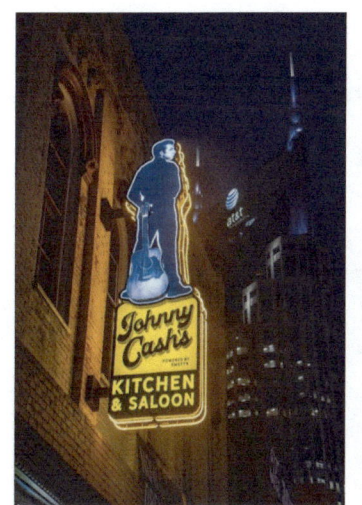

Sign outside Johnny Cash's Bar & BBQ & Grammy on display inside the Johnny Cash Museum – Photo Credits from left to right: Gabriel Torar & Kelly Lee Culbreth

5

FUN FACTS ABOUT... The Grand Ole Opry & Opryland Hotel

FUN FACT #17:

The Grand Ole Opry is not a venue. It is a show! And it has had six different homes since its debut in 1925.

The Opry bounced around between four different locations in downtown Nashville between 1925-1943.

In 1943, the show moved into the Ryman Auditorium, where it remained for over 30 years.

It was in 1974 when The Opry moved into its current and final home inside the Grand Ole Opry House.

* * *

FUN FACT #18:

A small circle was removed from the Ryman stage and embedded center stage in the new Grand Ole Opry House when it was first built in 1974.

Why? So everyone can stand in the same spot where country music legends once stood.

Stage inside the Grand Ole Opry House – Photo Credit: Jejim

* * *

FUN FACT #19:

The Guinness Book of World Records recognized the Grand Ole Opry as the "world's longest-running live music radio show."

In 1925, the show's original name was "WSM Barn Dance." In 1927, the name was changed to the Grand Ole Opry and has since become known as "country music's most famous stage." The Opry has inducted more than 200 members.

* * *

FUN FACT #20:

The Opryland Hotel opened in 1977 and was initially built to support the Grand Ole Opry House that moved to the area three years before.

Opryland Hotel indoor atrium – Photo Credit: Hendrickson Photography

Built on land next to the Opryland USA Amusement Park (which no longer exists), the hotel originally had 580 guest rooms and a ballroom.

* * *

FUN FACT #21:

After much expansion, the Opryland Hotel is now one of the world's biggest hotels and the largest non-casino hotel in the United States.

Today, the hotel offers 2,882 guest rooms and suites, an attached convention center with over 600,000 square feet of meeting space, an 18-hole golf course, over a dozen restaurants on site, and a gorgeous indoor garden with over 50,000 plants and a river running through it.

Opryland Hotel indoor garden and river – Photo Credit: Brewing Cats

* * *

6

FUN FACTS ABOUT... The Bluebird Cafe

Photo Credit: Lauren MacNeish

FUN FACT #22:

The Bluebird was opened to be a listening room for songwriters in 1982.

You don't go to The Bluebird just to hear live music. You go to listen to the writers sing their songs and tell the stories behind them. The club features acoustic music by both established and up-and-coming songwriters.

* * *

FUN FACT #23:

The Bluebird Cafe only seats 90 people but still receives over 70,000 visitors annually.

Because The Bluebird is such a famous location, many people are shocked at how small it is. But the intimate setting makes this live music venue a favorite among local songwriters.

With two shows a night, seven nights a week, and only 90 seats available, The Bluebird has standing room only at just about every show.

* * *

FUN FACT #24:

The club is famously known for its songwriters' "In The Round" format.

"In The Round" is a setting where the writers sit in the center of The Bluebird Cafe, taking turns playing their songs and telling their stories.

Songwriters have to audition for the honor of playing on this small stage.

* * *

FUN FACT #25:

The Bluebird Cafe has a strict etiquette policy while you are there. Patrons are required to remain silent during the performance of any songs.

You are only allowed to talk or applaud in between songs. Don't be surprised if you get a "Shhhh" from someone in the audience if you break this rule.

* * *

FUN FACT #26:

Future country star, Kathy Mattea, got a record deal in 1983 after playing regularly for a few months at The Bluebird Cafe.

The Bluebird had only been open for one year when Mattea got her record deal. However, because of Kathy's success, the venue became known among local musicians & songwriters as the best place to play in Nashville.

Also featured on the TV show "Nashville" from 2012 -2018, the venue became even more famous and well-known.

* * *

7

FUN FACTS ABOUT... Printer's Alley

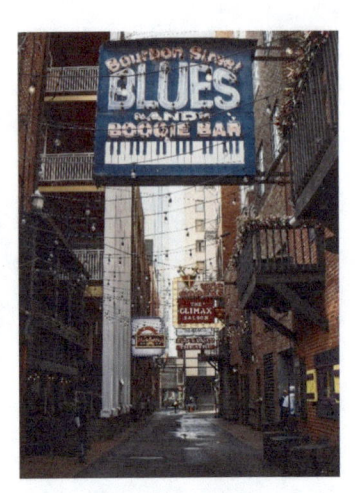

Printer's Alley from Church Street & Printer's Alley from Banker's Alley - Photo Credits from left to right: Cody Lannon & Brandon Jean

FUN FACT #27:

The oldest nightlife district in Nashville is "Printer's Alley."

The name comes from Nashville's deep history with the printing and publishing industries.

Sitting on two blocks between 3rd and 4th avenue in downtown Nashville, the Alley was home to two large newspapers, ten print shops, and 13 publishers in the early 1900s.

And over time, hotels, restaurants, and saloons moved into the area, making the Alley the center of Nashville's nightlife.

***

FUN FACT #28:

During Prohibition, many print shops in Printers Alley ran a series of speakeasies, creating a swinging underground bar scene.

After Prohibition was repealed in Tennessee in 1937, many of these bars stayed open. Some are still in business today!

***

FUN FACT #29:

Printers Alley was the city's red-light district, catering to men's secret desires from 1880-1914.

It was given the nickname, "The Mens' Quarter." Men could go there to grab some lunch, get a haircut, and enjoy the company of a working girl.

***

FUN FACT #30:

It is said that Printer's Alley is haunted.

In addition to two ghosts said to haunt Printers Alley that both tragically died in the same building, the Southern Turf, many swear they can also see and hear the ghost of David "Skull" Schulman walking around the Rainbow Room.

He was the owner of the Rainbow Room in the 1990s and was declared "The Mayor of Printers Alley" by the city council. Tragically, Schulman was attacked and murdered one night in 1998 while working alone in the club.

The club didn't reopen right away; the employees didn't want to go back in there. But after 17 years of being closed, the Rainbow Room, now called Skull's Rainbow Room, was reopened in 2015 by a local businessman.

* * *

FUN FACT #31:

Printer's Alley was also home to the city's first parking garage, first skyscraper, and several other historic buildings.

Printer's Alley Sign – Photo Credit: The Library of Congress

Although you will be hard-pressed to find any remnants of the printing business that established this bustling historic district of downtown Nashville, Printer's Alley is still a thriving area full of live music, clubs, restaurants, and entertainment.

* * *

8

FUN FACTS ABOUT... The Country Music Hall of Fame and Museum

FUN FACT #32:

In 2001, the Country Music Hall of Fame and Museum officially moved to 5th Ave., in the heart of downtown Music City, where it still resides.

The Country Music Hall of Fame first opened their doors in 1967. The original structure was a barn-shaped building located on Music Row. Over time, they outgrew the space and moved to their current location in 2001.

In 2014, the museum unveiled its $100 million expansion on 5th Ave, giving the structure a total of 350,000 square feet of space for its revolving exhibits, galleries, storage, retail stores, and event spaces.

The Hall of Fame continues to grow into one of Nashville's top tourist destinations.

* * *

FUN FACT #33:

The Country Music Hall of Fame and Museum's architecture was strategically thought out to resemble musical symbolism and elements of the industry.

Country Music Hall of Fame and Museum – Photo Credit: Sean Pavone

- When you stand in front of the building, the windows are meant to look like piano keys.
- There are round discs in the design that look like CDs and vinyl records.
- The tower in the rotunda imitates the diamond-shaped radio tower of WSM.
- And from the sky, the entire building is shaped like a bass clef.

FUN FACT #34:

Taylor Swift is a big part of the new Hall of Fame Museum.

In 2012, Swift donated $4 million to fund a new area of the museum, which is now called the Taylor Swift Education Center.

* * *

FUN FACT #35:

Nashville's 2010 Flood did some serious damage.

In 2010, less than a decade after moving to their 5th Ave location, a flood devastated several Nashville landmarks, including the Country Music Hall of Fame.

The mechanical room was flooded with more than five feet of water, and there was some damage to the Hall of Fame's beloved Ford Theater.

The flood was a setback, but the museum was still able to open its new expansion in 2014.

* * *

FUN FACT #36:

You can get married at the Country Music Hall of Fame.

Are you a BIG fan of country music? If so, the Country Music Hall of Fame and Museum can be the venue for your wedding day.

This architecturally stunning building hosts many private events throughout the year. In addition to boardrooms and event halls, the entire CMA Theater, which seats 776 people, can be rented for your special occasion.

But if you're a huge spender... There is also an option to rent the ENTIRE building for your event.

* * *

FUN FACTS ABOUT... THE COUNTRY MUSIC HALL OF FAME AND MUSEUM

Inside the rotunda of the Country Music Hall of Fame and Museum – Photo Credit: Matthew LeJune

* * *

9

FUN FACTS ABOUT... Lower Broadway

FUN FACT #37:

Lower Broadway in downtown Nashville is known as the "Honky Tonk Highway."

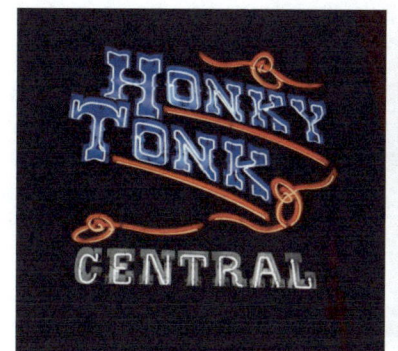

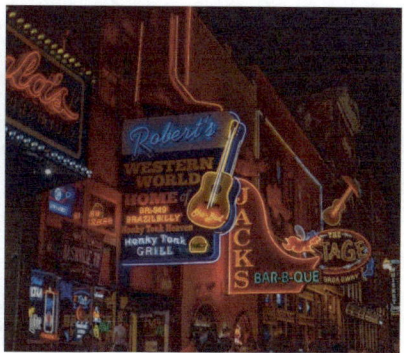

Photo Credits: Mana5280

What is a Honky Tonk? It is an establishment with cold drinks and a stage with music playing all day. And this popular strip of Broadway is full of them - with no cover charges and impressive roof-top bars.

Three hundred sixty-five days a year, some starting as early as 10 am, you can hear free, world-class music pumping from the many Honky Tonks lining this famous downtown street. You can't visit Nashville without spending at least one night doing a little "Honky Tonkin'" on Lower Broadway. **And don't forget to tip the musicians!**

FUN FACT #38:

The 2019 NFL Draft, held on lower Broadway in Nashville, was the most-attended draft in NFL history.

The event lasted for three days, and it was estimated that well over 600,000 people were in attendance.

Nashville beat out Denver, Kansas City, Las Vegas, and Cleveland for the bid to be the host city for the 2019 NFL Draft.

FUN FACT #39:

Nashville has become known as the "Bachelorette Capital of the World."

The masses travel to Lower Broadway to have a good time, including bachelorette parties. On any given night, you can see several groups of women throwing a party and celebrating the "bride-to-be" downtown.

Nashville businesses recognized the trend and began to cater to these "all-girl outings," and a new industry was born. As a result, there are countless activities and events geared towards your bachelorette fun, making Music City one of the hottest destinations in the world for your party.

* * *

FUN FACT #40:

The world-famous Tootsies Orchid Lounge is one of over 30 bars and honky tonks on Lower Broadway that play live music.

Though not as flashy as some of the other bars along this busy and crowded street, Tootsies is a legend in Nashville. History buffs will be impressed with the photo and memorabilia-filled walls. Originally called "Mom's," Tootsie Bess bought it in 1960 and renamed the venue to Tootsies Orchid Lounge after a worker painted the exterior purple.

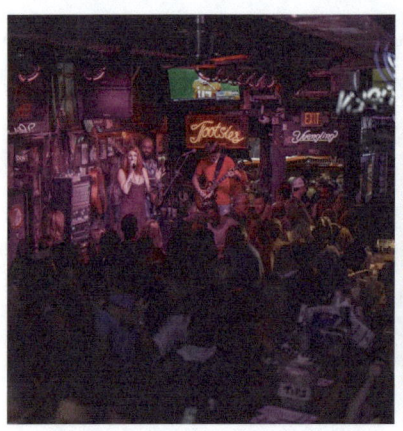

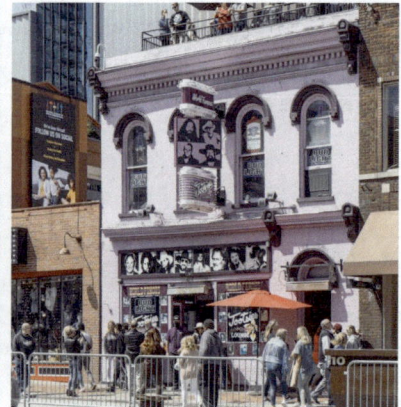

Photo Credits from left to right: Hari Nandakumar & Hendrickson Photography

In operation for over 60 years, this venue now has three stages that can host separate live music performances on each level, including a roof-top bar.

* * *

FUN FACT #41:

Or Not So Fun fact:

Historic 2nd Ave in downtown Nashville was severely damaged when a bomb detonated on Christmas morning in 2020.

Recovery of this historic district is still ongoing, with redevelopment creating new opportunities for downtown Nashville.

The city has been working hard to rebuild 2nd Avenue back to better than it was before.

* * *

10

FUN FACTS ABOUT... Other Music Venues

FUN FACT #42:

Nashville is a Live Music Venue Mecca with over 180 live music venues.

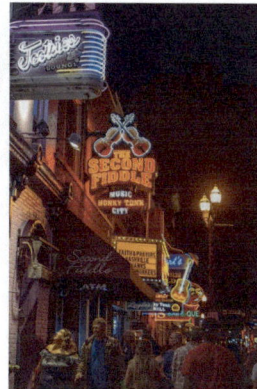

Photo Credits from Left to Right: Drew Hays, Mana5280, & Kelly Lee Culbreth

If a venue plays music for four or more nights a week, they are issued a guitar pick-shaped sign with the words 'Live Music Venue' on it.

* * *

FUN FACT #43:

The Wildhorse Saloon opened up in 1994 to capitalize on the line-dancing craze in the 90s.

Although the club still operates successfully as a bar and dance venue, it has also become a popular concert venue for all genres of music.

Located on historic 2nd Ave in downtown Nashville, this famous club has also been used to film TV shows, American Idol auditions, live events, and so much more.

* * *

FUN FACT #44:

The Schermerhorn Symphony Center was completed recently in 2006 but was designed to look like it has been there for decades.

Schermerhorn Symphony Center – Photo Credit: Jason Coleman

Some of the world's greatest concert halls were used as inspiration for the design of the building, which hosts a wide range of musical events that include all genres of music.

The building's main venue, the 1,844-seat Laura Turner Concert Hall, is one of the few halls in the nation to feature natural interior light through 30 special soundproof windows.

The building's name is in honor of the late Maestro Kenneth Schermerhorn, who led the Grammy Award-winning Nashville Symphony for 22 years.

* * *

FUN FACT #45:

Downtown you can enjoy a Broadway quality show at the Tennessee Performing Arts Center (TPAC), located one block from the State Capitol Building.

Founded in 1980, TPAC has four performance venues. The Andrew Jackson Hall, James K. Polk Theater, and Andrew Johnson Theater are located inside the Performing Arts Center building.

Across the street from the center is the fourth venue, the War Memorial Auditorium, a historic concert hall.

Broadway touring companies now consider Nashville a major market, allowing TPAC to offer a variety of memorable performances, musicians, comedians, dance companies, and Broadway shows.

Also in residence at TPAC are the Nashville Ballet, the Nashville Opera, and the Nashville Repertory Theatre.

* * *

FUN FACTS ABOUT... OTHER MUSIC VENUES

FUN FACT #46:

Nashville has an open-air concert venue downtown next to the Cumberland river called Ascend Amphitheater.

With the city skyline in the background, you can enjoy a concert while relaxing on a blanket or sitting in a lawn chair.

The Amphitheater is set inside the Metro Riverfront Park and has 2,300 fixed seats and room for 4,500 on the lawn.

View from Ascend's plaza & The John Legend concert on Sept 2nd, 2021 – Photo Credits: Kelly Lee Culbreth

* * *

11

FUN FACTS ABOUT... Things-To-Do

FUN FACT #47:

Andrew Jackson's Presidential Museum is not far from downtown Nashville and is one of the largest presidential homes open to the public.

Photo Credit: Library of Congress

The 7th President of the United States, Andrew Jackson, resided in Nashville until his death in 1845. His former home has been turned into Andrew Jackson's Hermitage Museum. The site covers 1,120 acres, with 30 buildings and even an on-site winery to visit.

* * *

FUN FACT #48:

Cheekwood Botanical Garden and Museum is a 55-acre historic estate located on the western edge of Nashville.

Cheekwood Mansion & Walkway in Botanical Garden – Photo Credits from left to right: Don (fallingwater123) & Dawn Hopkins

The 30,000-square-foot Cheekwood Mansion, inspired by the grand English manors of the 18th century, was first built in 1932.

The Cheek family lived at Cheekwood until the 1950s. Then in 1960, the property was turned into a beautiful Botanical Garden and impressive Art Museum which is still a popular destination for tourists and locals.

* * *

FUN FACT #49:

The General Jackson Showboat is one of the largest showboats ever built.

Sunset Cruise on the General Jackson Showboat – Photo Credit: Sean Pavone

Built by the largest inland shipbuilder in the United States, Jeffboat, the General Jackson was launched on the Ohio River in Indiana in 1985 to start the journey to its new home in Nashville on the Cumberland River. The Showboat holds over 1,000 guests and has four decks, including the Victorian Theater on the main deck. For most of the year, cruises depart daily from the Opryland Hotel. They last from 2.5 to 4 hours, and with views of the Nashville skyline, incredible performances, and authentic southern cuisine, this is a dinner show to remember.

* * *

FUN FACT #50:

The street art scene in Nashville is on fire! There are 29 (and growing) mind-blowing wall art murals.

Photo Credits from left to right: Lauren MacNeish, Katy Anne, & Caitlin Todd

With downtown art becoming a tourist attraction, several companies have popped up to help you view them all. So whether you do it yourself or hire someone to take you on a golf cart for a guided tour, you will have plenty of photo ops with this excursion.

Nashville may be known for music, but after this tour, you will see why the city's mural culture is exploding.

FUN FACTS ABOUT... THINGS-TO-DO

Legends Corner Wall Art – Photo Credit: Paul Brennan

Line for photo with popular wall art mural – Photo Credit: Ian Noble

* * *

FUN FACT #51:

You can tour one of the largest and wealthiest private estates in Nashville, the Belle Meade Plantation.

Belle Meade Mansion – Photo Credit: Melissamn

Now called the Belle Meade Historic Site & Winery, you can book tours of the grounds, which include a thoroughbred horse farm and on-site winery.

After a guided tour of the mansion, you can enjoy a complimentary wine tasting. There is also a walking trail, an on-site restaurant, a gift shop, and more.

* * *

12

FUN FACTS ABOUT... Annual Events

FUN FACT #52:

Tin Pan South, which takes place in Nashville annually, is the world's largest songwriter festival.

Every spring for five days, over 300 songwriters arrive in Nashville to play in venues all over town.

Photo Credits: Tim Mossholder

The songwriters love the spotlight, and the crowd gets to revel in experiencing each song with the person that wrote it. And during the festival, I'm sure a few songs are written too.

Tin Pan South is a great event to plan a trip to Nashville around. What a unique way to experience downtown and the music that you love.

* * *

FUN FACT #53:

Every year, the CMA Fest attracts country music fans from all over the world.

This is the ultimate experience for a country music lover!

In 1972, the event started as "Fan Fair" located inside the Nashville Municipal Auditorium. And about 5,000 fans would show up for live music and hope to get autographs from their favorite country music star.

Now called the CMA Fest, this event has grown into a 4-day extravaganza with over 300 performances on 11 official stages.

* * *

FUN FACT #54:

Nashville has become an in-demand destination for the 4th of July.

Every year, over 300,000 people (and growing) fill the streets of downtown Nashville to celebrate Independence Day. The main concert stage is located at the end of Lower Broadway, and there will surely be a stellar line-up of musicians and acts.

Lower Broadway on the 4th of July – Photo Credit: Garrett Hill

With a fireworks display that doesn't disappoint, food, drinks, and live music everywhere, it's no wonder Nashville draws so many people on the 4th of July.

* * *

FUN FACT #55:

Nashville knows how to throw a party for New Year's Eve!

Just like the 4th of July, hundreds of thousands of people fill the streets of Nashville to ring in the new year.

You can expect lots of venue options throughout Nashville and surrounding neighborhoods for great music and food to celebrate with your friends. In addition, there will be NYE parties happening in clubs and restaurants all over town.

But the main event, which is broadcast live, happens on Lower Broadway. And all evening long, the concert stage will be full of one well-known act after another.

At midnight, there is a countdown with the signature Music Note Drop, followed by an impressive fireworks display set to live music.

* * *

FUN FACT #56:

Every year, the historic Five Points District in East Nashville hosts a costume art festival dedicated to the tomato.

The Tomato Art Fest is a 2-day festival and concert that is free to attend, and costumes are encouraged!

People from all over attend to enjoy fun tomato-themed art, live music, great food, wacky contests, and a little shopping. There are activities for the kids, and they even elect a King and Queen Tomato to lead the parade featuring a brass band.

It is considered to be one of the city's premier hipster events.

* * *

13

FUN FACTS ABOUT... Food & Restaurants

FUN FACT #57:

Nashville is often called the "Hot Chicken Capital of the World," and that hot chicken is said to have been derived from a plot for revenge.

Back in the 1930s, a man named Thornton Prince was supposedly out late one night, possibly up to no good with another woman. To get revenge, Prince's lover at home purposely over-seasoned his fried chicken with hot spices. But to her avail, he loved it and opened up a chicken shack to serve the concoction to the locals.

The hot chicken dish became very popular and is now said to have been invented and started in Nashville.

Hot chicken sandwich - Photo Credit: Blake Guidry

* * *

FUN FACT #58:

The "Meat & 3" is another southern tradition that started in Nashville.

A Meat & 3 restaurant will present its customers with their choice of meat and then the option to select three sides to go with it. And there are usually a lot of options to pick from.

If you eat at a restaurant like this, you better be ready for some good ole southern cooking!

* * *

FUN FACT #59:

The Loveless Cafe has become so popular they are now making up to 10,000 biscuits a day!

In 1951, husband and wife Lon and Annie Loveless started the Loveless Cafe to serve families and travelers scratch-made southern meals along Highway 100 just south of Nashville. Their homemade dishes became so popular they turned their home into a restaurant and 14-room motel.

Fast forward to today, and this eatery has grown. There are now additional buildings to provide space for one-of-a-kind weddings, celebrations, meetings, and much more.

Photo Credit: James R. Martin

Welcomed by an iconic neon sign, more than half a million visitors stop in to savor a home-cooked meal every year. The Loveless Cafe has stayed true to its southern roots over the years and continues to attract locals and tourists.

* * *

FUN FACT #60:

The Pancake Pantry, located in Nashville's hip Hillsboro neighborhood, is so popular that it is a regular occurrence for a line to form around the building.

The locals say it is worth the wait. The restaurant serves up the best pancakes using a long-time family recipe. Not only is their batter made fresh daily, but they also make their syrup fresh every day too!

* * *

FUN FACT #61:

Nashville isn't just about hot chicken, southern cuisine, and Meat & 3s. Fine dining restaurants with elegant atmospheres, exquisite chef-inspired food, and fine wines can be found all over the city.

However, it is highly recommended that you make reservations in advance. Especially if you want to try a specific restaurant featured on one of those "Top 10 Fine Dining" lists you saw online.

*＊＊

14

FUN FACTS ABOUT... Sports in Nashville

FUN FACT #62:

Nashville's professional football team is the Tennessee Titans.

October 26, 2014 - Nashville Titans vs. the Houston Texans - Photo Credit: Grindstone Media Group

Previously known as the Houston Oilers, the team moved to Nashville in 1997 and called themselves the Tennessee Oilers.

But in 1999, in response to fan requests, they changed their name to the Tennessee Titans. A name that was chosen to reflect power, strength, leadership, and other heroic qualities.

That same year, they played a memorable season, making it to Super Bowl XXXIV on January 30, 2000.

* * *

FUN FACT #63:

Music City's professional hockey team is the Nashville Predators.

The "Preds," a term used by locals, became members of the National Hockey League in 1998. On any given game night, downtown is buzzing with Predator hockey fans wearing their yellow and navy jerseys.

March 30, 2022 - Photo Credit: EQRoy

Nashville's hockey games are known for being some of the loudest games in the league. And, of course, you can expect only top-notch live music during the intermissions.

The Predators won one conference championship in 2017.

* * *

FUN FACT #64:

In December 2017, a Major League Soccer franchise was awarded to Nashville. Known as the Nashville Soccer Club, it was in 2020 that this team began playing league games inside Nissan Stadium.

In May 2022, Nashville's brand new 30,000-seat soccer stadium, **Geodis Park,** opened up. Built on the historic Nashville Fairgrounds, Geodis Park is the largest stadium dedicated to soccer ever built in the United States and Canada.

The team is principally owned by John Ingram of Ingram Industries, along with other partial investors.

* * *

FUN FACT #65:

For fans of college sports, Nashville's Vanderbilt University is a Division 1 school.

The Commodores, as they are known, play in the Southeastern Conference or SEC.

The Vanderbilt football stadium has a capacity of 40,550 and is located in the heart of campus. Named Dudley Field, it was the first stadium in the South to be built exclusively for college football.

* * *

FUN FACT #66:

Nashville has a minor-league baseball team called the Nashville Sounds.

The name came from the city's association with the music industry. The team plays its home games at Herschel Greer Stadium, which opened in 1978 and holds 10,052 baseball fans.

The stadium's best-known feature is a giant 115 ft guitar-shaped scoreboard.

The Sounds moved up to a Triple-A level in 1985 and serve as a farm club for six major league franchises.

* * *

15

FUN FACTS ABOUT... Bridgestone Arena

Bridgestone Arena at night – Photo Credit: Chait Goli

FUN FACT #67:

Bridgestone Arena is home to the NHL's Nashville Predators.

Besides hosting the Predators, the arena is a popular venue for concerts, award shows, figure skating championships, basketball tournaments, other sporting events, bull riding, comedy shows, children's events, and so much more.

* * *

FUN FACT #68:

Completed in 1996, Bridgestone Arena has a seating capacity of 17,159 up to 20,000, depending on the event and set-up.

* * *

March 27, 2022 - Photo Credit: Kelly Lee Culbreth

FUN FACT #69:

Claims have been made that Bridgestone Arena is one of the loudest arenas in sports.

According to a Purdue University study, the noise inside the arena can reach levels that rival a military jet airplane during takeoff (130 decibels) or a clap of thunder (120 decibels).

FUN FACT #70:

Many well-known events have taken place in Bridgestone Arena.

- In 2003, the Predators hosted the NHL Entry Draft.
- In 2016, it was the location for the NHL All-Star Game.
- In 1997, the venue hosted the United States Figure Skating Championships.
- In 2004, the USA Gymnastics National Championships was held here.
- Nine times between 2015 and 2025, the arena served as a primary venue for the SEC men's basketball tournament.
- In 2014, the NCAA Women's Final Four was played in Bridgestone.
- Since 2006, the Country Music Association (CMA) Awards have been held in this arena.

To name a few.

FUN FACT #71:

The Grammy Nominations Concert was held at Bridgestone Arena in 2012.

This event kicks off the Grammy season with live performances and the revealing of the nominations. This was the first time the event took place in a city outside of Los Angeles.

* * *

16

FUN FACTS ABOUT... Nissan Stadium

Photo Credit: Gabriel Tovar

FUN FACT #72:

Located on the east bank of the Cumberland River, Nissan Stadium is the home field for the NFL's Nashville Titans.

With a seating capacity of 69,143, the highest in Nashville, the stadium is often used for major events, concerts, shows, sporting events, the CMA Fest, and more.

Some of those events include:

- the annual Music City Bowl
- the CMA Fest in June of every year
- Major concerts by artists such as The Rolling Stones, Garth Brooks, Elton John, Billy Joel, Guns N' Roses, Beyonce, Taylor Swift, the Red Hot Chilli Peppers, and so many more

FUN FACT #73:

To kick off the 20th year in Nashville, in 2018, the Tennessee Titans put two 20th anniversary logos in each end zone.

The uniforms also got an upgrade, and the field yard line numbers were changed to match the number style on the new team jerseys.

* * *

FUN FACT #74:

Built in 1999, Nissan Stadium has been given several names:

- Adelphia Coliseum (1999-2002)
- the Coliseum (2002-2006)
- LP Field (2006-2015)
- Nissan Stadium (2015 - current)

* * *

FUN FACT #75:

During the flood of 2010, six feet of water filled the stadium's playing surface and reached into the player's locker rooms.

In addition to repairing the flood damage, Nissan Stadium received numerous upgrades in 2012, including two brand new LED video displays measuring 157 feet by 54 feet that were installed in each end zone and, at the time, were the 2nd largest displays in the NFL.

* * *

FUN FACT #76:

In 2022, the Titans paused any future renovations on the stadium to explore the possibility of building a new facility in the near future.

Later that year, they released renderings for their new stadium, with hopes of opening in 2026.

The designs include an enclosed dome, a projected seating capacity of 55,000-60,000, and 170 luxury suites.

*　*　*

17

FUN FACTS ABOUT... Music City Center

FUN FACT #77:

For $623 million, Nashville built a new 2.1 million-square-foot Convention Center in 2013, so the city could host large city-wide conventions in the downtown area.

Front of Nashville's Music City Center – Photo Credit: 4kclips

Called the **Music City Center**, adding this architecturally stunning building to downtown has created a significant economic benefit for the greater Nashville area by attracting local and national events.

* * *

FUN FACT #78:

Located adjacent to Bridgestone Arena and the Country Music Hall of Fame, the Music City Convention Center sits on 16 acres.

The building also has an extensive outdoor border of green space next to the Country Music Hall of Fame, which is used for outdoor concerts and events.

Right in the heart of the area known as SoBro, the Convention Center is surrounded by hotels, restaurants, and entertainment venues.

* * *

FUN FACTS ABOUT... MUSIC CITY CENTER

FUN FACT #79:

With 350,000 square feet of exhibit space, Music City Center provides many options for events, large or small.

In addition to the extensive exhibit space, the Convention Center also has:

- 90,000 square feet of meeting room or break-out space
- A Grand Ballroom that is 57,500 square feet
- The Davidson Ballroom: 18,000 square feet
- 5,000 square feet of retail space
- 60 meeting rooms
- 32 loading docks

* * *

FUN FACT #80:

The Music City Center is a certified Gold Level LEED building. An award given by the U.S. Green Building Council, LEED stands for Leadership in Energy and Environmental Design.

The Convention Center is committed to reducing environmental stress by integrating sustainable practices into day-to-day operations and being more energy efficient.

In addition to waste reduction and recycling policies, the Center also has:

- 4 acres of Green Roof
- 845 Solar Panels
- a 360,000-gallon water collection tank

FUN FACTS ABOUT... MUSIC CITY CENTER

Top of Music City Center with 4 acres of green roof - Photo Credit: Felix Mizioznikov

* * *

FUN FACT #81:

Music City Center is home to over 100 pieces of public art that were purchased from or commissioned by local artists.

During the planning stages, the Convention Center had a budget of $2 million for interior and exterior art.

Over 225 artists submitted applications, and pieces were chosen featuring a broad spectrum of artistic styles and mediums, including paintings, suspended pieces, new media, mosaics, light works, and eight commissioned site-specific monumental pieces.

A total of 52 artists are represented in the Center's art collection.

* * *

18

FUN FACTS ABOUT... Landmarks

FUN FACT #82:

The Parthenon in Nashville's Centennial Park is the world's only full-scale replica of the original Greek temple in Athens.

Photo Credit: Agnieszka

Just west of downtown Nashville, the Parthenon is the centerpiece of Centennial Park. Completed in 1925, it operates as an art museum today. Inside the Parthenon, there is a 42-ft-tall statue of Athena. It is the largest indoor statue in the western hemisphere.

Bonus fun fact: A McDonald's flag pole was used to create the statue's spear.

* * *

FUN FACT #83:

The Tennessee Capitol Building is located in downtown Nashville and is one of the oldest capitol buildings in the United States that is still in operation.

Photo Credit: Travis Saylor

The tomb of James K. Polk, the 11th president of the United States, is on the capitol grounds. Also entombed above the structure's cornerstone is the capitol's designer, William Strickland. Built between 1845 and 1859, Strickland thought this building was his crowning achievement.

* * *

FUN FACT #84:

Located on the Campus of Belmont University, the Belmont Mansion was the largest house built in Tennessee before the Civil War.

Photo Credit: Steve Heap

The mansion was constructed between 1849-1860 by Adelicia and Joseph Acklen. It is one of the few homes still standing in Nashville that was built in the 1850s.

Full of Civil War history and thought of as one of the most architecturally significant houses of the 19th Century, the mansion is now a landmark that is open to the public for tours, or you can book your upcoming event there.

* * *

FUN FACT #85:

The Music City Walk of Fame Park is a city landmark paying tribute to those connected to Music City who have contributed to the world through music and songs from all genres of music.

Located across the street from the Country Music Hall of Fame and Museum, this public park sits on the lawn of the Hilton in downtown Nashville.

Stars made from granite line the walkway honoring legendary figures from Nashville's music industry. You can stroll the Walk of Fame, find your favorite artists, and take pictures. It's even extra special if you catch one of their induction ceremonies.

* * *

FUN FACT #86:

Bicentennial Capitol Mall State Park is a 19-acre urban state park located just north of the Capitol Building.

This beautiful Tennessee State Park has walkways, monuments, and memorials. There is also a 2,200-seat amphitheater used for special events.

The cornerstone for the mall was laid in 1994. And as a part of Tennessee's 200th anniversary of statehood celebration, the mall was dedicated in 1996 by then Governor Don Sundquist and Vice President Al Gore.

Used by downtown dwellers and visitors to the city as a relaxing green space, the State Park is also an excellent venue for farmers' markets, art festivals, and craft fairs.

FUN FACTS ABOUT... LANDMARKS

Inside the Bicentennial Capitol Mall State Park, there are clusters of Tennessee flags on each end of the River Walk, located behind the Tennessee State Capitol Building. Photo Credit: Brandon Hooper

* * *

19

FUN FACTS ABOUT... Downtown Nashville

FUN FACT #87:

Did you know downtown's AT&T building is also called the Batman Building?

Take one look at it, and you will know why.

Photo Credits from left to right: 12019 & Cesar G

This building, completed in 1994, forever changed the Nashville skyline. Rising 617 feet in the air, this 33-story skyscraper known as the Batman Building is currently the tallest in the state of Tennessee.

* * *

FUN FACT #88:

In 2022, Nashville brought in over $9 billion from visitor spending.

Nashville continues to break tourism records with sold-out hotels, a happening nightlife, and busy restaurants.

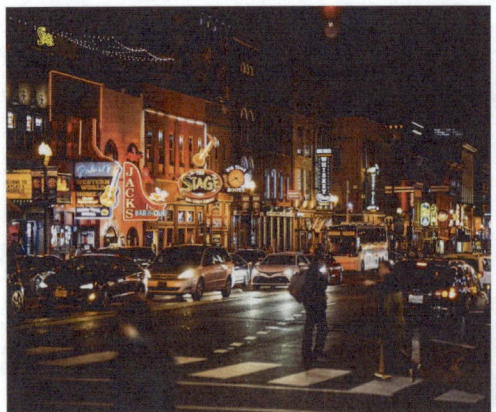

Lower Broadway, otherwise known as, "Honky Tonk Highway" - Photo Credits from left to right: Chad Morehead & Ushindi Nanegabe

To keep up with demand, the city, expecting up to 15 million visitors in 2023, has continued to develop and build up the downtown area to keep that momentum going.

* * *

FUN FACT #89:

Downtown Broadway is home to the only museum in the nation dedicated to the impact of African American music.

USA Today named the **National Museum of African American Music** (NMAAM) the "Best New Museum in 2021."

Photo Credits: Kelly Lee Culbreth

With self-guided tours, it will take around 90 minutes to walk through the vast collection of stage costumes, instruments, sheet music, recording equipment, and photographs from many genres.

* * *

FUN FACT #90:

The well-known Demonbreun Street in downtown was named after Nashville's "first citizen," Timothy Demonbreun.

Photo Credit: Paul Brennan

Timothy took refuge in a cave along the Cumberland River around 1769 after being attacked by Indians. He permanently settled in Nashville in 1790 until he died in 1826.

The cave is now listed on the National Register of Historic Places and is privately owned.

FUN FACT #91

SoBro, which stands for "South of Broadway," is an up-and-coming downtown area known for all things new.

This part of the city has enjoyed significant improvements over the last decade or two. The Country Music Hall of Fame, the Schermerhorn Symphony Center, the new sprawling Nashville Convention Center, and the Johnny Cash Museum are just some of the attractions in this neighborhood on the south side of Broadway.

With multiple live music venues, major hotel brands, spas, restaurants, bars, retail shops, and boutique properties, SoBro has a little of everything.

* * *

20

FUN FACTS ABOUT... Nashville Universities

FUN FACT #92:

Nashville has quite a few higher learning institutions. Some of the more well-known collages in or around the downtown area are:

- Vanderbilt University
- Belmont University
- Tennessee State University
- Fisk University
- Lipscomb University
- Bethel University
- Meharry Medical College
- The Nashville School of Law

* * *

FUN FACT #93:

Founded in 1873 and sitting on 333 acres in the heart of Nashville, Vanderbilt University is currently ranked #13 in "National Universities" by the U.S. News and World Report.

Vanderbilt University West End Tower – Photo Credit: The Library of Congress

"Vandy" was started with a $1 million gift from "Commodore" Cornelius Vanderbilt and is now a private research university with ten schools that resides on a beautiful campus.

One of those affiliate schools is the Vanderbilt University Medical Center which partners with Vanderbilt Hospital, located right next to campus.

FUN FACT #94:

In 2021, for the 13th consecutive year, Belmont University was included on the list of "Most Innovative Schools" by U.S. News & World Report.

Belmont University has a long list of accolades, making it one of the most prestigious schools in the southeast.

Belmont's campus resides on 93 acres and is located just a few blocks from downtown.

Bonus Fact: Based on a suggestion from music legend Roy Acuff, Professor Robert E. Mulloy began offering an Introduction to Music Business course in 1971. That course was the beginning of what would become Belmont's globally known Music Business Program, launching many successful careers in the music and entertainment industry.

* * *

FUN FACT #95:

Established in 1912, Tennessee State University is the only state-funded historically black university in Tennessee.

Offering undergraduate, graduate, and doctoral degrees, the main campus sits on 500 acres just 10 minutes northwest of downtown Nashville.

Their 2nd campus, the Avon Williams Campus, is located directly downtown near the business and government district.

TSU used to be called the Tennessee Agricultural & Industrial State College until they changed the name to Tennessee State University in 1968.

* * *

FUN FACT #96:

Founded in 1866, Fisk University is the oldest higher learning institution in Nashville, according to U.S. News and World Report.

Fisk University's Jubilee Hall - Photo Credit: The Library of Congress

By 1871, the college was in severe debt. So, they raised everything they had to finance a fund-raising concert tour featuring the school's Fisk Jubilee Singers. As mentioned before, this was the first ever worldwide tour of a singing group and sparked the beginning of Nashville becoming known as a city full of music.

A highly ranked historically black school, Fisk University sits on 40-acres minutes from downtown and is considered a historic district by the National Register of Historic Places.

* * *

21

FUN FACTS ABOUT... Miscellaneous Stuff

FUN FACT #97:

Class of 1971, Oprah Winfrey graduated from East Nashville High School and was voted "most popular."

While in high school, Oprah began broadcasting on Nashville's WVOL radio. Soon after, at 19, she became the youngest person AND the first African-American woman to anchor the news at Nashville's WTVF.

In 1987, she graduated from Tennessee State University with a degree in Speech and Performing Arts.

* * *

FUN FACT #98:

Launched in 1912, The Goo Goo Cluster was invented in Nashville and became America's first combination candy bar.

Made of caramel, marshmallow, peanuts, and milk chocolate, this candy bar is iconic. The name is believed to stand for the "Grand Ole Opry" and can be found all over the city.

This picture was taken from inside the Johnny Cash Museum Gift Shop, with the Goo Goo Clusters store across the street on 3rd Ave. Photo Credit: Kelly Lee Culbreth

* * *

FUN FACT #99:

President Theodore Roosevelt coined the phrase "good to the last drop" after drinking a cup of local coffee at the Maxwell House Hotel in Nashville.

The phrase was used as an advertising slogan for Maxwell House Coffee, which was served at and named after the hotel.

Both the coffee brand and the hotel are still in operation today.

* * *

FUN FACT #100:

The country's first seeing-eye dog school was in Nashville.

In 1928, Morris Frank, a blind student at Vanderbilt University, traveled to Germany to train and bring back what would become his seeing-eye dog named Buddy.

Soon after, in 1929, Frank helped found The Seeing Eye in Nashville, the country's first guide dog school.

* * *

And last but not least...

FUN FACT #101:

Three presidents have called Nashville home:

- Andrew Jackson
- James K. Polk
- Andrew Johnson.

* * *

22

Miscellaneous Photos

View of the Nashville Skyline – Photo Credit: Kelly Lee Culbreth

Nashville Riverfront on the Cumberland River – Photo Credit: Matthew Jungling

MISCELLANEOUS PHOTOS

Album wall inside the Johnny Cash Museum & Public Square Park at the top of 2nd Ave – Photo Credits: Kelly Lee Culbreth

Light Meander Sculpture in Riverfront Park & Lower Broadway taken from Acme Feed & Seed's roof-top on 1st Ave – Photo Credits: Kelly Lee Culbreth

Aerial view of Nashville's skyline & Dogwood lined street in the SoBro neighborhood – Photo Credits from left to right: Ginger Colwell & Kelly Lee Culbreth

Nashville, TN skyline taken from the east bank of the Cumberland River – Photo Credit: Garrett Hill

Recording Studio vocal booth in Nashville, TN – Photo Credit: Paulette Wooten

Wall Art on 2nd Ave – Photo Credit: Paul Brennan

Willie Nelson Museum – Photo Credit: Paul Brennan

Inside the Willie Nelson Museum – Photo Credit: Paul Brennan

MISCELLANEOUS PHOTOS

The General Jackson Showboat on the Cumberland River in front of Nissan Stadium – Photo Credit: Kelly Lee Culbreth

Line for Hattie B's Hot Chicken next to Bridgestone Arena – Photo Credit: Kelly Lee Culbreth

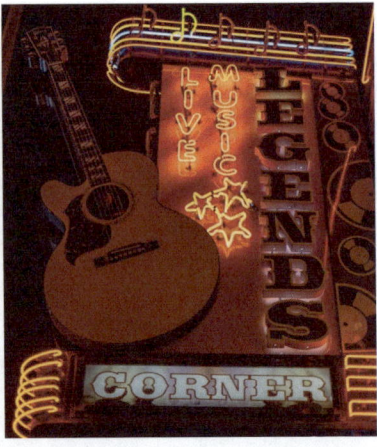

Johnny Cash Museum on 3rd Ave & Legends Corner on Broadway – Photo Credits from left to right: Nathan Mullet & Mana5280

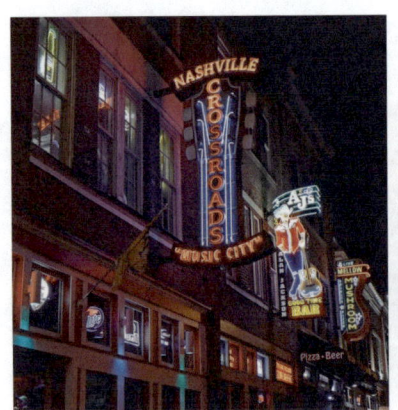

Nashville Crossroads & AJ's on Broadway. AT&T Batman Building photographed from the east bank of the Cumberland River – Photo Credits from left to right: James Anthony & Cesar G

MISCELLANEOUS PHOTOS

The Parthenon inside Centennial Park – Photo Credit: Kevin Abbott

Nashville skyline with Bridgestone Arena – Photo Credit: Brandon Jean

23

Conclusion

Nashville may have started with humble roots in music, printing, and trade, but it has become one of the fastest-growing cities in America and shows no signs of slowing down anytime soon.

It takes more than one visit to truly experience all that Nashville offers. Centering your trip around a concert, game, or special event is a great place to start. Then spend the rest of your time enjoying the honky tonks, world-class restaurants, museums, roof-top bars, and other attractions all over the city.

And if you are a local reading this book, I encourage you to try something NEW you haven't experienced. It is easy to keep falling in love with this city over and over again. With so much to see and live music all over the city, it's no wonder Nashville is a popular destination for tourists and locals.

Now.... Y'all come visit Music City soon!

CONCLUSION

* * *

If you found "101 Fun Facts About Nashville, TN" interesting, entertaining, or useful, please leave a favorable review for the book on Amazon. It is always appreciated, and authors love hearing from their readers.

* * *

24

References

About Fisk University. (n.d.). Fisk University. Retrieved January 22, 2023, from https://www.fisk.edu/about/

Andrews, E. (2023, January 20). *10 Things You May Not Know About Davy Crockett.* HISTORY. https://www.history.com/news/10-things-you-may-not-know-about-davy-crockett

Art | nashvillemusiccitycenter.com. (n.d.). https://www.nashvilleconventionctr.com/about/art-collection

Auditorium, R. (n.d.-a). *Johnny & June: Love within the Ryman Walls.* Ryman Auditorium. https://www.ryman.com/news/detail/johnny-and-june-love-within-the-ryman-walls

Auditorium, R. (n.d.-b). *Why is Ryman Auditorium So Famous?* Ryman Auditorium. https://www.ryman.com/news/detail/why-is-ryman-auditorium-so-famous-

REFERENCES

Augustyn, A. (2011, April 8). *Nashville Predators | History & Notable Players*. Encyclopedia Britannica. https://www.britannica.com/topic/Nashville-Predators

Awards & Accolades. (n.d.). Belmont University. Retrieved January 22, 2023, from https://www.belmont.edu/about/accolades.html

Belmont History. (n.d.). Belmont University. Retrieved January 21, 2023, from https://www.belmont.edu/about/history/index.html

Belmont Mansion | Nashville Historic House Museum |. (n.d.). Belmontmansion. https://www.belmontmansion.com/

Carr, C. (2022, March 31). *10 Interesting Facts About the Country Music Hall of Fame*. The Boot. https://theboot.com/country-music-hall-of-fame-facts/

Castello Cities Internet Network, Inc. (2022, June 7). *History of Nashville*. Nashville.com. https://www.nashville.com/history-of-nashville/

Cheekwood Botanical Garden and Museum of Art Facts for Kids. (n.d.). https://kids.kiddle.co/Cheekwood_Botanical_Garden_and_Museum_of_Art

Demoyne, M. (2022, May 17). *25 Amazing Facts About Nashville*. TravelAwaits. https://www.travelawaits.com/2398171/25-amazing-facts-about-nashville/

Downtown's 5 Best Historical Facts We Bet You Didn't Know | Downtown Nashville. (n.d.). https://nashvilledowntown.com/post/downtowns-5-best-historical-facts-we-bet-you-didnt-know

Editorial Team. (2022, June 20). *15 Most Famous Nashville Nicknames.* Find Nicknames. https://www.findnicknames.com/nashville-nicknames/

Eveline, E. (2022, February 17). *Why Did Nashville Become the Home of Country Music?* Journeyz. https://journeyz.co/nashville-home-of-country-music/

Fest Flashbacks. (2022, August 4). CMA Fest 2023. https://cmafest.com/history/

Fields, F. (2023, April 20). *Quick Facts.* Vanderbilt University. https://www.vanderbilt.edu/about/quick-facts/

Fox, M. (2023, January 16). *2023 Belle Meade Guided Mansion Tour with Complimentary Wine Tasting.* Tripadvisor. https://www.tripadvisor.com/AttractionProductReview-g55229-d12639147-Belle_Meade_Guided_Mansion_Tour_with_Complimentary_Wine_Tasting-Nashville_Davidson_.html

Guttery, C. (2022, July 31). *29 Murals in Nashville: A Practical Guide to Mind-Blowing Art.* Wayfaring Views. https://wayfaringviews.com/nashville-murals-guide/

Hawker, A. (2023, January 12). *Must-Visit Nashville Bars on Broadway - 2023.* Nashville to Do - Exploring Nashville & Tennessee. https://nashvilletodo.com/ultimate-guide-to-the-best-broadway-bars-in-nashville/

REFERENCES

Johnson, C. (2023, January 19). *Nashville breaks tourism records in 2022 with nearly $9B brought in from visitor spending.* News Channel 5 Nashville (WTVF). https://www.newschannel5.com/news/nashville-breaks-tourism-records-in-2022-with-nearly-9m-brought-in-from-visitor-spending

Kollar, L. (2017a, January 25). *A Brief History of How Nashville Became "Music City."* Culture Trip. https://theculturetrip.com/north-america/usa/tennessee/articles/a-brief-history-of-how-nashville-became-music-city/

Kollar, L. (2017b, March 24). *A Brief History of Printers Alley, Nashville.* Culture Trip. https://theculturetrip.com/north-america/usa/tennessee/articles/a-brief-history-of-printers-alley-nashville/

Kraft, M. (2016a, April 4). *11 Facts About Nashville You Never Knew Were True.* OnlyInYourState®. https://www.onlyinyourstate.com/tennessee/nashville/nashville-facts/

Kraft, M. (2016b, September 19). *12 Incredible, Almost Unbelievable Facts About Nashville.* OnlyInYourState®. https://www.onlyinyourstate.com/tennessee/nashville/incredible-facts-about-nashville/

Lastoe, B. C. S. (2019, May 2). *There's a new bachelorette capital, and it's not Vegas.* CNN. https://edition.cnn.com/travel/article/bachelorette-party-nashville-tennessee/index.html

Leimkuehler, M. T. T. (2020, February 7). *Pollstar names Ryman Auditorium "Theater of the Year" for 10th consecutive year*. Nashville Tennessean. https://eu.tennessean.com/story/entertainment/music/2020/02/07/pollstar-awards-ryman-auditorium-wins-theater-honor/4692056002/

Let Freedom Sing! Music City July 4th. (2022, November 16). Visit Nashville, TN. https://www.visitmusiccity.com/july4th

Loveless Cafe History, Videos, and Happenings. (2020, May 13). The Loveless Cafe. https://www.lovelesscafe.com/about/history/

Micky, M. (2022, August 3). *vanderbilt stadium capacity - Stadium Capacity*. Stadium Capacity - Check Here Updated 2022. https://stadiumcapacity.com/vanderbilt-stadium-capacity/

Music City Center in Nashville. (2021, April 21). Visit Nashville TN. https://www.visitmusiccity.com/meetings/music-city-center

Music City Walk of Fame Experience | Nashville Walk of Fame | VisitMusicCity.com. (n.d.). https://www.visitmusiccity.com/walkoffame/experience.htm

Nashville River Cruises | General Jackson Showboat. (2022, November 7). General Jackson. https://generaljackson.com/

Nashville Symphony. (n.d.). https://www.nashvillesymphony.org/about/Schermerhorn-Symphony-Center

REFERENCES

Nealon, T. (2020, June 10). *The Ghosts of Printers' Alley | Haunted Printers' Alley*. Ghost City Tours. https://ghostcitytours.com/nashville/haunted-nashville/printers-alley/

Old Town Trolley Tours. (2020, November 20). *Fun Facts About Nashville*. https://www.trolleytours.com/nashville/facts

Old Town Trolley Tours. (2022a, September 11). *Printer's Alley Nashville History & Travel Tips*. https://www.trolleytours.com/nashville/printers-alley

Old Town Trolley Tours. (2022b, October 19). *Music Row Nashville Information Guide*. https://www.trolleytours.com/nashville/music-row

Oprah Winfrey. (1954, January 29). IMDb. https://www.imdb.com/name/nm0001856/bio

Organ, M. T. T. (2017, June 4). *Bridgestone Arena decibel levels soar for first Stanley Cup Final*. The Tennessean. https://eu.tennessean.com/story/sports/nhl/predators/2017/06/03/predators-noise-level-bridgestone/368172001/

Our Story. (n.d.). Tomato Art Fest. https://www.tomatoartfest.com/ourstory

Sc, N. (n.d.). *GEODIS Park | NashvilleSC.com*. Nashville SC. https://www.nashvillesc.com/geodispark/about-geodis

Second Avenue | Downtown Nashville. (n.d.). https://nashvilledowntown.com/go/second-avenue

Sewell, A. (2021, December 6). *20 Fun Facts About Nashville, TN, You May Not Know*. Destguides. https://www.destguides.com/united-states/tennessee/nashville/nashville-tennessee-facts

Snapp, L. (2020, April 17). *10 Surprising Facts About The Grand Ole Opry*. After MidNite With Granger Smith. https://aftermidnite.iheart.com/content/2020-04-17-10-surprising-facts-about-the-grand-ole-opry/

Staff, U. T. (2023, January 21). *The History of Opryland Hotel*. USA TODAY. https://eu.usatoday.com/

Sustainability | nashvillemusiccitycenter.com. (n.d.). https://www.nashvilleconventionctr.com/about/sustainability

Tennessee Performing Arts Center. (2022, December 5). *About*. Tennessee Performing Arts Center®. https://www.tpac.org/about/

The Story of Music City. (2022, September 7). Visit Nashville TN. https://www.visitmusiccity.com/explore-nashville/music/story-music-city

Tremblay, C. (2022, May 4). *10 Fascinating Facts About the Ryman Auditorium*. The Boot. https://theboot.com/ryman-auditorium-facts/

Vanderbilt University. (n.d.). U.S. News & World Report. Retrieved January 22, 2023, from https://www.usnews.com/best-colleges/vanderbilt-3535

REFERENCES

Visit Nashville. (n.d.). Belmont University. Retrieved January 22, 2023, from https://www.belmont.edu/visitnashville/index.html

Webb, S., & Rose, D. (2022, October 10). *15 interesting facts about Nashville, TN - NASHtoday | Your Resource for All Things Nashville, TN*. NASHtoday. https://nashtoday.6amcity.com/15-interesting-facts-about-nashville-tn

Wiki Targeted (Entertainment). (n.d.). Baseball Wiki. https://baseball.fandom.com/wiki/Nashville_Sounds

Wikipedia contributors. (2022a, May 25). *Wildhorse Saloon*. Wikipedia. https://en.wikipedia.org/wiki/Wildhorse_Saloon

Wikipedia contributors. (2022b, September 3). *Bicentennial Capitol Mall State Park*. Wikipedia. https://en.wikipedia.org/wiki/Bicentennial_Capitol_Mall_State_Park

Wikipedia contributors. (2022, August 7). *Music City Center*. Wikipedia. https://en.wikipedia.org/wiki/Music_City_Center

Wikipedia contributors. (2022c, September 19). *AT&T Building (Nashville)*. Wikipedia. https://en.wikipedia.org/wiki/AT&T_Building_(Nashville)

Wikipedia contributors. (2022d, November 6). *Bluebird Café*. Wikipedia. https://en.wikipedia.org/wiki/Bluebird_Caf%C3%A9

Wikipedia contributors. (2022e, December 22). *Parthenon (Nashville)*. Wikipedia. https://en.wikipedia.org/wiki/Parthenon_(Nashville)

Wikipedia contributors. (2022f, December 23). *Fisk University.* Wikipedia. https://en.wikipedia.org/wiki/Fisk_University

Wikipedia contributors. (2023a, January 11). *Nissan Stadium.* Wikipedia. https://en.wikipedia.org/wiki/Nissan_Stadium

Wikipedia contributors. (2023b, January 13). *Future Tennessee Titans Stadium.* Wikipedia. https://en.wikipedia.org/wiki/Future_Tennessee_Titans_stadium

Wikipedia contributors. (2023c, January 16). *Nashville SC.* Wikipedia. https://en.wikipedia.org/wiki/Nashville_SC

Wikipedia contributors. (2023d, January 18). *2019 NFL Draft.* Wikipedia. https://en.wikipedia.org/wiki/2019_NFL_Draft

Made in United States
Troutdale, OR
06/18/2025